**PEARL
BOOKS**

Published by Pearl Books, LLC
1000 Pearl Road Pleasantville, TN 37033

Written by Debi Pearl
Illustrated by Michael and Debi Pearl

Reprinted by arrangement with The Heirs to the Estate of
Martin Luther King Jr., c/o Writers House as agent for the
proprietor New York, NY.

listentomydreambook.com

Printed in the U.S.A.

Listen To My Dream may be purchased at a special discount
for schools, universities, gifts, promotions, fund raising,
or educational purposes. Special editions can be created
for those honoring the memory of
Dr. Martin Luther King, Jr.

For information regarding permission to reprint or for purchases,
contact Mel Cohen, Managing Partner, Pearl Books, LLC
1000 Pearl Road Pleasantville, TN 37033
931-593-2484 Email: **melcohen@hughes.net**

LISTEN TO MY DREAM

Written by Debi Pearl
Illustrated by Michael & Debi Pearl

"Mama Dear,
Why am I black?
And why do I have to be at the back:
the back of the bus,
the back of the store,
the back of the room,
even the back door?
And why do I have to look at the floor?
I wanna look up,
I wanna be seen,
I want to be as proud as a King!"

Born January 15, 1929 and raised in Atlanta, Georgia

Listen, little brother, to my dream.
I dreamed a man as white as I am black
bowed to me and shook my hand
and said to me,
"Please take the stand."
And when I stood
and began to speak,
golden words came out of me.
"Up, you mighty race"
Come march with me
declaring our rights and liberty.
And we did march,
and we did win.
I hope I dream this dream again.

"Up, you mighty race" quote from Marcus Garvey (1887-1940)

Peace

Freedom

Honor

Rights

Dignity

Equality

There are some words I need to know.
Big words, neat words: words to show
how man should stand for what is right.
I gotta study with all my might
I must prepare my dream to share.
There's folks that need me
waiting out there.

His school teacher, Miss Lemon, from Oglethorpe Elementary
inspired her students to take pride in their heritage.

You say, my son,
you have a dream;
then listen close to me.
You must be kind,
you must be true,
you must be brave
when danger threatens you.
To wait and wait
and wait some more,
never discouraged,
never cast down.
Let peace be your helper,
let peace be your plan,
let peace be your message,
and with peace you will win.

Years passed but nothing changed.
our God-given rights
weren't ours to claim.
But the dream lived on
as the boy grew to be
a preacher man
his destiny decreed.

He spoke out loud,
he spoke out clear
to all of those
who chose to hear,
"I have a dream;
A Freedom Dream!
We as a people
must be bold
to claim our rights,
to take our stand,
to march on
to Freedom Land!"

**Pastor of Dexter Avenue Baptist Church
Montgomery, Alabama (1954-60)**

He gave the people
strength of heart.
He made them be as one.

He led the march
that led to the start
of dignity and honor for everyone.

But bitter words
and angry hearts
caused many to rebel.
The law was wrong
and they were right.
It made them mad,
they started to fight.
He called for peace
but they would not heed,
he was going much to slow.

So blood was shed and
men were dead.

"Stop!" He cried,
"This is not right.
You must believe in me."

The people saw hate's final end
and believed in the preacher once again.
But on the preacher the blame was laid,
so back to jail he went again.

In the midst of turmoil
his soul in deep despair,
behind the bars of unjust law,
he wrote his letter there.
"I have finished with my waiting,
the time to march is now.
My people have done their suffering
and there is no more they should bear.
I have a dream.
We share that dream.
The victory's almost here!"

Birmingham Jail   April 16, 1963
"The Letter"

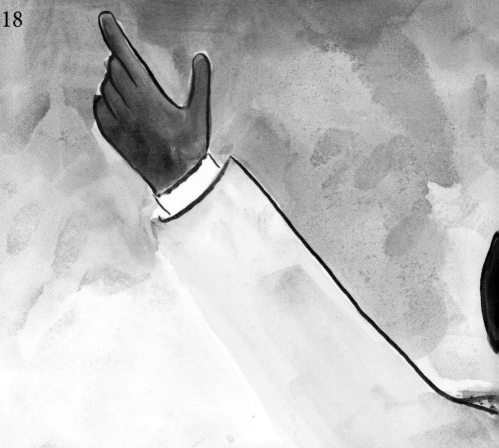

He charged on to battle,
never looking back.
He gave a thousand speeches
and led most every march.
When his body was tired and weary,
when his own family did without,
he gave his very soul and being,
and in the cold darkness
a ray of light was felt.

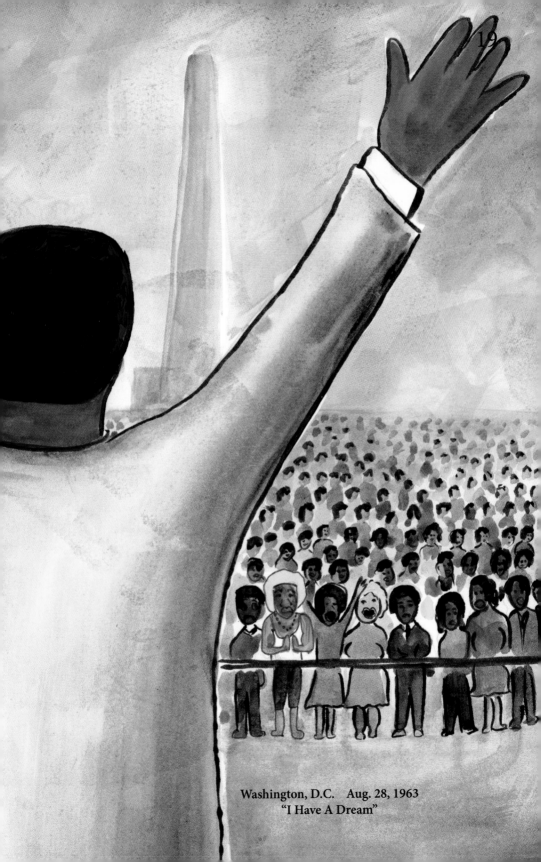

Washington, D.C.   Aug. 28, 1963
"I Have A Dream"

At home he was an outcast -
a rebel rousing man.
But the world looked on
with different eyes
and saw a noble man.

NOBEL PEACE PRIZE
Dec. 1964

Then in the height of struggle
with his strength now at its end,
came the world's highest honor
from the world's wisest men.
With this shiny bit of metal
and rolled up parchment scroll,
they declared he had a message
that really should be told.

SCLC

Civil Rights Movement
Poor Peoples' Campaign
Ebenezar
University of Mississippi
Soldier's Field July 1966
Riverside Church
Operation Bread basket

He worked just that much harder.
His dream was coming true.
The hardest battle he'd ever fought
he had won and so had you!

Southern Christian Leadership Conference

"I have been to the mountain.
I have seen the Promised Land.
It is ours for the taking.
It's a mighty fine land.

"We have done this thing together.
We have marched hand in hand.
Although I'd like to be with you
as you go possess the land,
I just might not make it to that
glorious, wholesome stand.

"But for my children I have given
the greatest gift a man can give.
I have given them a heritage -
my life was spent doing this.
It's called dignity and freedom.
It's called liberty for every man.
And now each one must do his part
to become a better man.
The victory's there just waiting.
Come, claim the land."

Mason Temple Memphis, TN
April 3, 1968   "I've Been To The Mountaintop"

The next day as he was hurrying
to serve his brothers
in Memphis, Tennessee,
a cruel and ruthless killer
lay in wait across the street.

The preacher stepped out of the door
to tell the singer man
to sing the song he loved so well,
"Precious Jesus, Take My Hand."
And as he uttered these simple words
before he could turn to go,
a shot rang out and the preacher fell
dead upon the floor.

Shot and killed April 4, 1968
Memphis, Tennessee

The people's hearts were broken.
Hate grew on every hand,
but out of this great turmoil
you could almost hear him say,
"Please forgive your brother,
do this just for me.
I gave my life for this great cause,
now carry on with dignity.
Only one race has been won.
There is still so much to be done."

3 ½ Mile Funeral Procession
Atlanta, Georgia   April 9, 1968

Now sometimes in the evening
when the cool spreads o'er the land,
I hear children's happy voices,
I see his mark on every hand.
I know that he is with us
enjoying this Freedom Land.

His dream became his passion,
his passion our release
from the years of degradation,
from the years of misery.
We have risen!
We are Free!
So is he!

lest children

we

forget

Tribute to a King

Every once in a while, down through the pages of time, the life and works of one man forever changes the lives of millions of people. Martin Luther King, Jr. was such a man.

The great continent of Africa is the birthplace of the black race. It is a huge land where elephants and giraffes, cheetahs and lions freely roam, and a varied host of vibrant black people groups have lived there for thousands of years.

About 350 years ago, on the other side of the world from Africa, a new nation was being forged in liberty. This new land was called America. People looking for land and freedom came to America from all over Europe, and some even came from Asia and established huge farms and factories. This new country did not have enough people to help bring in the harvests of the big farms or to work the factories.

Wicked seamen who knew of the land called Africa promised the farmers that they would bring strong slaves. These evil men sailed their ships to Africa and with the help of corrupt tribal leaders began kidnapping thousands of young unsuspecting Africans. By the 1700s the markets of America were selling strong black men and beautiful black women to labor in the fields. For many long years the slave market was legal in America.

Most people knew it was wrong and some tried to do something to end the practice, but things continued as they were. Finally, in 1865, toward the end of a terrible Civil War, President Abraham Lincoln signed the 13th Amendment making it illegal to own another human being.

Although their legal status changed, few black people were allowed to enjoy the fruits of liberty. The slave owners, fearing the consequences of allowing their slaves to learn to read, had not allowed the slaves any education. The freed slaves now found themselves without land, no place to live, no money, unable to read, and denied participation in the political process. Many evil white people still treated the black people like slaves and were even very cruel to them. Most of the ex-slaves ended up working on the same plantations, doing the same labor as before, for very low wages that left them in poverty.

Yet even in the midst of these terrible injustices a few black men and women gained an education and dedicated their lives to educating their people. Schools, colleges and other institutions of learning were established, but to the average black child these special places were unknown.

Ninety years after being freed, most black people still worked as domestic servants or were forced to take low paying jobs. There were laws called Jim Crow Laws that restricted Blacks from many fundamental liberties. A black person was not welcome in most restaurants or parks, nor could they drink from a water fountain unless it was marked For Colored. It was the same for restrooms. All black people were told to sit at the back of the bus or in the back seat of cars when they rode with white people.

Everyone knew it was wrong to treat people like this, but only a few people, black or white, were willing to speak up. Those few brave souls were often cruelly treated, some unto death.

In 1955, one chilly December day in Montgomery, Alabama, a tired black lady who had spent her day sewing some white ladies' clothes got on a city bus. She walked slowly to the middle of the bus and sat down. The bus made several stops picking up more and more white people. When all the front seats were full, the driver told Rosa Parks, "Get up and give your seat to that young white man."

Rosa was surely afraid, but she said, "No. It is my seat and I will not move." It was a big moment in time. She took a chance on being arrested, beaten or even worse, but she had suffered humiliation and injustice for too long. The police were called and Rosa Parks was arrested. Rosa didn't know, at that time no one knew, that this was the beginning of the civil rights movement.

Though Rosa Parks must have felt all alone, she was not. There were thousands of people just waiting for someone to tell them what they could do to make a difference.

History was in the making. The young man you read about in this book was now 26 years old and ready for the challenge. He spoke with authority and wrote with eloquence. He was knowledgeable in history and acquainted with law, and he knew how to turn this bad situation to good. His heart yearned to break the bonds that had enslaved his brothers and sisters. His name carried the title he had earned—Dr. Martin Luther King, Jr.

The day Rosa Parks was arrested, a lawyer phoned Dr. King asking him to organize a bus boycott. The time was right. Dr. King, together with other dedicated men, planned a massive boycott of the Montgomery buses. Dr. King told the people, "Don't ride the buses. Find another way to work or walk. They will miss the money they get from us riding their buses. We must do this together or we will not be successful."

For days the buses ran down the roads almost empty. No Blacks rode the bus even if it meant walking great distances to work. Dr. King told the city leaders that the buses would stay empty until Negroes were allowed to sit wherever they pleased on the buses and not be forced to give up their seats to white people. The massive loss of revenue caused the city of Montgomery to allow Blacks to ride their buses with dignity, sitting where they pleased. This victory gave the people courage. They saw that if they were willing to make an effort they could effect change. It was the beginning of many successful boycotts and sit-ins.

A year later the United States Supreme Court finally ruled that the Jim Crow Laws violated the United States Constitution. Dr. King's leadership had helped win a great battle against segregation, but the war had really just begun.

Martin Luther King, Jr., was born January 15, 1929. His father was a preacher, and his mother, Alberta, was a teacher. Martin's mother taught him how to read before he started school. Their house was always full of books, which he read with relish. Martin's father was a kind, hard-working pastor that helped many people find jobs. He was a good example for his son. Young Martin finished high school when he was only 15 years old. Then he went to Morehouse College. After graduating he traveled to Pennsylvania to study at Crozer Theological Seminary. He graduated with honors and went on to Boston University, where he earned a doctorate. That is where he met the beautiful Coretta Scott, who he married in June of 1953. Dr. King had many opportunities for jobs, but he knew he could lead his people best if he were a preacher. In 1954 he became the pastor of Dexter Avenue Baptist Church in Montgomery, Alabama.

The following year he received the phone call about Rosa Parks. From that day on Dr. King was a very busy man, leading marches, making speeches, writing, and organizing the people to work peacefully as one strong voice. He was arrested 30 times, stabbed, and received many death threats. He worried for his family's safety, yet he moved forward as one driven by a mission.

In 1963 he was chosen Man of the Year by Time Magazine. On August 28, 1963, Dr. King and other leaders led a march into Washington D.C. Over 250,000 people marched from the Washington Monument to the Lincoln Memorial. It was there that Dr. King gave his memorable speech, *I Have a Dream*. It was voted the best speech of the 20th century. In 1964 he received the Nobel Peace Prize. He met with Presidents Eisenhower, Kennedy, and Johnson. The whole world had come to know and respect this man that had united the African American people to peacefully bring forth such a great change in so short a time.

Then one warm spring day, April 4, 1968, in Memphis, Tennessee, evil finally found its mark. That morning he stepped out onto the balcony of his motel, ready for his next task. A gunman, an escaped convict hiding in an adjacent building, took careful aim then pulled the trigger. At only 39 years old Dr. Martin Luther King, Jr. was shot dead. Grief took on new meaning when the man of hope and vision was taken. For days angry people rioted, looted, and raged in bitterness. Then the anger gave way to an intense sadness and terrible loss.

At the funeral Dr. Ralph Abernathy, a good friend of Dr. King's, told the grieving people, "This is one of the darkest days of mankind." The funeral procession was a three and a half mile walk from Ebenezer Baptist Church to Morehouse College with more than 100,000 mourners that included dignitaries from all over the world. In death his body was carried to its resting place in an old farm wagon pulled by two mules--a testament to his humble life of service.

Without Dr. King's peaceful kingly leadership, the Civil Rights Movement fractured, but the brilliant work he had done in an amazingly short period of time had brought dignity and justice for millions of people. His dream would become the vision for all who toiled under the load of oppression, his words would ring out to each new generation, and the work he had started would continue to grow.

Once he was a little boy with a big idea. His name was Martin Luther King, Jr. He worked hard, studied long and watched carefully in order to prepare himself to make his impossible dream a reality. Today all boys and girls can be or do anything they are willing to work for…because he made the way.

What about you? Do you have a dream?

I Have A Dream

I have a dream that one day this nation will rise up and live out the true meaning of its creed: "We hold these truths to be self-evident: that all men are created equal."

I have a dream that one day on the red hills of Georgia the sons of former slaves and the sons of former slave owners will be able to sit down together at the table of brotherhood.

I have a dream that one day even the state of Mississippi, a state sweltering with the heat of injustice, sweltering with the heat of oppression, will be transformed into an oasis of freedom and justice.

I have a dream that my four little children will one day live in a nation where they will not be judged by the color of their skin but by the content of their character.

I have a dream today.

I have a dream that one day, down in Alabama, with its vicious racists, with its governor having his lips dripping with the words of interposition and nullification; one day right there in Alabama, little black boys and black girls will be able to join hands with little white boys and white girls as sisters and brothers.

I have a dream today.

I have a dream that one day every valley shall be exalted, every hill and mountain shall be made low, the rough places will be made plain, and the crooked places will be made straight, and the glory of the Lord shall be revealed, and all flesh shall see it together.

Martin Luther King, Jr. August 28, 1963

About the Author

Debi and her husband, Michael Pearl, are international best-selling authors together having sold over a million books. Their books have been translated into over 30 languages worldwide. They author a free bi-monthly magazine called No Greater Joy which explores child training, marriage, Bible teaching, and natural healing. You are invited to visit them at *nogreaterjoy.org* and *debipearl.com*.

Other books by Michael and Debi Pearl

Available From No Greater Joy Ministries
nogreaterjoy.org

Created To Be His Help Meet – Good and Evil Graphic Novel
Holy Sex – To Train Up a Child
Available in English and Spanish

No Greater Joy Volumes 1, 2, and 3 – The Help Meet's Journey
Available in English

Available From Pearl Books, LLC
Listen To My Dream
listentomydreambook.com

The Vision
debipearl.com